My Dear Liberia
Recollections
Poetic memoirs from my heart

Ophelia S. Lewis

Published by
Village Tales Publishing
P. O. Box 1059
Pine Lake, GA 30072-1059

www.villagetales.com

ISBN: 0-9753609-0-6

Printed in the United States of America
By Morris Publishing

DEDICTION

This book is dedicated to every Liberian, whether through birth, naturalization or adaptation. It is devoted to the memories of those lives lost and to those victimized by our ruthless civil war. It is my wish that for the bloodsheds on Liberia's soil, we must always be indebted to them that from this time forth; Liberia must stand for liberty and justice for all.

In loving memory of my Grandmothers

Mary Yeke-Thorpe
and
Martha A. Harris

*"When God accompanies you,
your steps are eliminated"*

African Parable

Liberia's National Anthem

Lyrics: Daniel B. Warner, 1847
Music: Olmstead Luca, 1860

All Hail, Liberia Hail!
This glorious land of liberty
Shall long be ours.
Though new her name,
Green be her fame,
And mighty be her powers,

In joy and gladness
With our hearts united,
We'll shout the freedom
Of a race benighted,
Long live Liberia, happy land!
A home of glorious liberty,
By God's command!

All hail, Liberia, hail!
In union strong success is sure
We cannot fail!
With God above
Our rights to prove
We will o'er all prevail,

With heart and hand
Our country's cause defending
We'll meet the foe
With velour unpretending
Long live Liberia, happy land!
A home of glorious liberty,
By God's command!

*"The lizard who threw confusion
into his mother's funeral rite,
did he expect outsiders to carry
the burden of honoring his dead?"*

African parable

FOREWORD

We humans have the ability to adjust to suffering, no matter how difficult. Take for instance during the era of slavery when Africans in North America were dehumanized to worthlessness. They survived, otherwise there would be no African-Americans in the United States today. Likewise, the Jews survived Hitler's brutality. Liberians are no different. We too have survived the self-destructive arena of violence against our own. Despite those consequences, *Time* ought to be use for healing – God has provided for us that possibility. It *must* start with each person.

Who among us does not have a story to tell or emotions to share? Liberia was the home of folks who loved one another. We enjoyed peace. We honored our elders. We took care of strangers and we ensured the well being of our children. We were a multi-culture people brought together for the sole purpose to enjoy freedom. We were no different than people in other parts of the world who consists of the *have's* and the *have not's*. We resembled all societies on God's green earth. All of our fingers are not equal, aren't they?

I have no apology for my ever-so-quick assessors who will deny themselves the joy of the past and rather choose to continue to hate for whatever reason. These are memories from my heart, written to begin my own healing. I only wish to share them with you and hope that you get out of this book the only purpose for which it was written – that it inspires you to begin your own healing. May peace be upon us. God bless Liberia!

Ophelia S. Lewis

Contents

"The fly that has no one to advise him follows the corpse into the ground"

African parable

The **Palm Tree** represents the source of the Liberian product, palm oil, which has greatly enriched our land. The **Wheelbarrow** represents the work of our fathers who cleared the forests to plant crops. The **Shovel** represents the hard work of miners, the mineral wealth in the Liberian hills. The **White Dove carrying a scroll** in its beak represents peace and the scroll represents wisdom and knowledge coming to the new nation, Liberia. Across the sea, **a Rising Sun,** a sign of a new republic rising in the world. The **Sailing Ship** represents the coming of the first colonists from America.

"The boy, who persists in asking
what happened to his father
before he has enough strength to avenge him,
is asking for his father's fate"

African parable

Monrovia
A small city with a big heart!

Whether rich or poor, people in Monrovia knows how to have a good time. Close your eyes and think for a moment. Even if you've never been to Monrovia, some images will probably be made up by your imagination: Hot sun or heavy rainfall, spicy food and music, highlife music, the uplifting and irresistible sounds of West Africa on ELBC. On any given day, one can enjoy the smell of salt seawater off Cooper's beach or tour the beautiful boundary coconut trees down the shores of Coconut Plantation. There are paved sidewalks throughout the crowded city with merchants selling traditional flavoring of roasted corn-on-a-cobs, sizzling plantains or delicious cassavas right off their glooming fire coal-pots. Or perhaps a friendly market woman would roll a piece of old newspaper into a small funnel for your fresh roasted ground-peas (peanuts) measured in an old blue Vicks's container. That will cost you only about twenty-five cents. Better yet, you might prefer the refreshing juice from the neatly peeled oranges sold for fifteen cents. The effort put into those crafty lines carved on the orange skin alone should cost fifty cents, but art is in the blood of all Africans. These women are more than happy to dress their fruit than simply peeling off the skin.

Monrovia, with its commanding view of the Atlantic ocean on two sides, has no stylish skyscrapers or sophisticated subways. Nevertheless, life in this city is pleasing. If you need to catch a movie, ask any Monrovian on Broad Street to point the way to a cinema. He might need to know your preference before directing you to Gabriel or Roxy or Rivola cinema. Gabriel's billboard will display Hollywood's latest film, Roxy will most likely be playing Asia's best marshal art films and Rivola will be screening India's heartwarming romantic movies. Who wouldn't enjoy two movies for a dollar and fifty cents at any of those cinemas? While in Sinkor the classy Relda cinema hosts uppity Monrovians who would rather catch one movie at night - they pay a higher fee too. There are other cinemas throughout Monrovia; these were my favorites.

There may not be glitter and glamour, so to speak, but a city would not be a 'city' without merriment. At night Monrovia has a place for anyone who wants to satisfy their desire for the bar or the club. Whether you visit the elegant lounge of Hotel Africa or Vicky's Spot in Logan Town, or any local "shop" bar for that matter, everybody will leave merry. A bar in New York City stocked with drinks of every kind will have no more on its shelves than a popular club or lounge in Monrovia. You can very well have any brand name liquor that you want. Besides the famous local brewed Club Beer, certain clubs will satisfy your taste for imports such as Heineken, Beck's, Guinness Stout, as well as American brews: Budweiser, Miller, Coors and the likes. Local shops will stock Club Beer along with schnapps, palm wine (liquor from the palm tree) and cane juice (liquor from the sugar cane plant). Soft drinks - Coca-Cola, Fanta, and Club Muscatel - are also found in these establishments. There's a drink for everyone.

Want to shop? Visit Sinkor Shopping Center on Tubman Boulevard or A to Z Supermarket on Camp Johnson Road. How about Charlotte's Supermarket on the Old Road or better yet, Island Supermarket across the bridge? You may pick up a birthday gift along with some wrapping papers from GITCO on Broad Street.

A beautifully designed V finger-ring or a set of earrings from the local goldsmith will make a good impression. They will say, "you na cheap". Liberians love gold!

The busiest shopping area is down Waterside. Waterside is comprise of many stores, stocked with provisions of every kind, on both sides of the streets. Lebanese and Syrian businessmen own most of these establishments. One would find any item; from cloth to household appliances. In fact, most of the shopping is done there before going to the mission (*boarding school*). If my memory serves me right, there must have been at least two hundred stores in that shopping area.

For that out-of-the-blue shopping, make a run to "the shop". In Africa, it is expected that the host provide refreshments for their guests. When someone is visiting your home, your parents will send you to "the shop" to buy Coca-Cola, Fanta or Ginger ale and a pack of tasty Coconut biscuits or Tuc biscuits, or perhaps a tin of Jacobs' Cream Crackers for the entire family. Remember Hard Tac biscuit? It is an essential item in any chop box for 'mission children'. It comes in handy for those hungry times when the dinning hall is close.

Some people satisfy their hunger with a cold bottle of Coca-Cola and a loaf of Fanti bread. It is flavorsome when some Blue Band margarine is spread on. My brother, Aaron, told me of his own on-the-spot remedy for hunger at the football field – crackers and condense milk. Energy. Sugar shock. Need I say more? That should keep you going like the Energizer Bunny.

'The shop', in every community throughout Monrovia, is visited daily. As a matter of fact, it is visited at least three times a day per average household. I know now that it were the smart business people (Nigerians and Ghanaians) who own those local shops.

Besides going to 'children show', which is catching a matinee at your favorite cinema, Sophie's ice cream parlor was a much-loved venue for children and grownups alike. A trip to Sophie's was my favorite pastime. I enjoyed their chocolate-covered ice cream bars the most.

Liberians are religious, whether Christian or Muslin. Remember WWP? For those of you who do not know or can't remember, that's *wake*, *wedding* and *party*. We always celebrated festivities as well as mourned someone's passing with close cooperative spirits. Every community heard the sad news of someone's passing over the airwaves of either ELBC or ELWA radio stations. Most wake-keeping took place in the homes which lasted the entire night until morning. We sang and prayed with bereaved relatives and friends. Fresh coffee and home-made biscuits were served. Besides, there was always extra help in getting your home ready for wake-keeping. The house got a fresh coat of paint, the yard was cleared (*grass cut*) and in some cases large rocks, skillfully placed throughout the yard, were whitewashed. This was some form of decoration. For a long time I associated the smell of fresh paint to mourning.

We carried out funeral services in the church and at times, would march behind the hearse from the churchyard to the gravesite on Center Street; whether it was S.D.A. church on Camp Johnson Road or Providence Baptist Church on Broad Street.

Most weddings took place on Saturdays. Was that one of those self-imposed laws? Just kidding.I do believe that people did get married only on Saturdays. Joll-of-rice, potato salad, variety of cakes, drinks, and other foods would be served in outrageous quantity. Liberians love to party!

Where else to go? Prominent venues in Monrovia: Color Spot (*to have your glamour pictures taken*), Abi-Jaoudi or A to Z (*supermarkets*), Auriole Enterprises (*school uniforms*), Agip, Shell or BP (*service stations*) King Burger (*for hamburgers, French fries and shakes*), Rooster and Diana Restaurants (*first-rate dinning*), Mandarine (*Chinese food*), Ducor Inter-Continental (*upscale hotel lounging*) or Hotel Africa (*Los Vegas style accommodates*), Lipps, Katiio or Bacardi clubs (*New York style nightclub*), Y.E.S. (*car rental*), Anderson or Grace's (*Funeral homes*), Lutheran Church in Sinkor, Jehovah's Witness' Kingdom Hall, the Mosque around Newport Street area, Methodist Church on Ashman Street, Episcopal Church on Broad Street, Cathedral Church on Crown Hill or Mother Dukley's Faith Healing Temple across the bridge (*places of worship*).

Monrovia, a small city with a big heart!

I am Thinking of Liberia

As the day chase away the night
And the night chase away the day
Homesickness has made a nest in my heart
And sits there like a bird
I am thinking of Liberia!

Liberia is painted in my heart
Her red earth
Her green jungle
Her silver drops of tropical rainfall
Her red hibiscus dotted on green bushes

In the silence of her countryside
I hear the cries of her Pepper Birds
I yearn to touch the chill in her air
So pleasantly refreshing after the heavy rain

I hear the whispers of her night
That rides along the wind from the Atlantic
I hope it finds its way into my mind
I am thinking of Liberia!

Her son,
Running and rolling an old rim-less tire
Her daughter,
Plating the hair of a corncob
Pretending that it is her baby

Her woman's gracious walk
In her colorful lappa
That trails royally behind her
Her man, draped with a special robe
That only he may wear

Her mother, whose infant
Sleeps cozily against her back
Her father, standing waist-deep
Among straw-yellow rice in its ripeness

I crave the warmth of her sun
To beat against my shoulders
While I walk down the winding road
Through richly cultivated sugarcane farm

My memory is kind to me
Although it is only a taste of a lesser satisfaction
As the day chase away the night
And the night chase away the day
Liberia is painted in my heart
I am thinking of Liberia!

The Bus Ride

A *'hold-it! hold-it!'* (Renault bus) will almost certainly never take you to the Old Road; it runs from across the bridge or down Waterside to the Airfield. The carboys on the Renault buses were not as sophisticated as the carboys on the Toyota buses. For some reason, they were a little more reserved. I think it was because of the bus; perhaps the style and/or the structure. The Renault bus was shorter and took fewer passengers while the Toyota bus was longer and carried more passengers.

I did not appreciate the way the carboys insisted on seating six persons for seats built for four. We Africans tend to accept self-imposed laws by those we depend on. Because there were no government public transportations, we accepted the rules given to us by the drivers whose buses we depended on for transportation.

Passengers entered a Toyota bus on the right side of the bus while the door of a Renault bus was at the back. Its double door swings open; often times the carboy remains sitting as the passenger boards, then the bus simply takes off. Booooring! Quite, dull. Contrary to those boring Renault carboys (*I'm truly sorry boys*), a carboy on the Toyota bus dramatically hops off the bus before it comes to a complete stop and before taking off, he bangs on the side of the bus to let the driver know that it is time to take off. These clever carboys jog a few yards along side the moving bus before skillfully jumping on. They hang one leg out the door for a moment or so, before finally closing the folding door. Dramatic! Absolutely cool.

At that time, we paid fifteen cents for a bus ride. Beside your means of transportation, you are in for a treat. You will be entertained by the theatrics of passengers getting on and off the bus. It would not matter which bus you have boarded.

Possibly the plot of a group of youngsters who boarded the bus together will begin to unfold as soon as the first person in that particular group gets off the bus. "My friend, behind there, will pay for me", he or she will inform the carboy. No one in particular at the back of the bus will acknowledge this responsibility; however the bus takes off with the carboy's anticipation of getting paid by the next passenger who, it would seem, is associated with the passenger that got off. The bus soon stops at a passenger's request. "Bus stop!" A passenger gets off, pays only fifteen cents and before you know it, an argument erupts. The carboy insists on getting paid for the passenger that got off moments before, however, the individual denies accepting the responsibility. After a moment or so, the driver becomes impatient and takes off slowly – fifteen cents is not much to waste valuable time. He does not want to risk losing passengers waiting on the first available bus at the next bus stop. If it's a guy, the carboy will remark an insult about the boy's mother. If it's a female, he will refer the insult directly to her. For some reason, it seem more gratifying to these carboys to use terminology of the female's anatomy offensively when expressing their discontent.

The carboys keep the coins collected as fares in a small towel held in their hands. How they kept all those coins from falling out of the washcloth remains a mystery to me.

Eager peddlers are always at the bus stop. To make a quick sale, they rush around each window of the bus to advertise their goods.

"Popcorn, here! Popcorn, here! Popcorn, here!"

"Boil eggs! Boil eggs!"

Or, "Sweet mother! Sweet mother!" These are assorted colorful frozen Kool-Aid in plastic sandwich bags. Actually they are home-made popsicles. You could also purchase cold water, which is appreciated on a hot day. It is convenient to buy a snack without getting off the bus. You can get a pack of Juicy fruit or Chicklets, peppermint candy or toffee.

There are nicknames given to certain bus stops. When it is intended for the bus to stop at the John F. Kennedy Memorial Hospital, the carboy would yell, "Just for killing" - *not an ideal name for a hospital, in my opion.* Or, the Maternity Center bus stop on Capital By-pass, the carboy would yell, "Baby factory!" People exit the bus at those stops not necessarily because of the nicknames; everybody is aware that these carboys are show-offs.

Those bus-rides through the streets of Monrovia made good memories for a lot of people. When a jam-packed bus would yet pick up another passenger, an old woman for that matter, who is tired and eager to get home, or the driver just don't mind squeezing in another "fifteen cents". Someone would voluntarily offer his seat to her. "Old Ma, come sit down-o." Liberians tend to end sentences with *'o', 'ah', 'eh'* or *'eh-so'*.

Today, I wouldn't mind one of those bus-rides. Conceivably I might catch the bus from Logan Town, change bus down Waterside (Get off a Renault and board a Toyota), sit in my favorite seat, the carboy's seat, which is the single seat just to the left as you enter the bus. That way I get to see every passenger that boards. I might know someone. I also enjoyed the carboys' flashy performances, especially their jumps on and off the bus. I will buy ten cents worth of peppermint candies (*my favorite*) and a pack of Juicy fruit. I wouldn't mind the frequent stops traveling those fifteen somewhat miles from Water Street to Broad Street, then on to BTC area before heading to United Nations Drive. We will pass thru Bassa Community and head on to Tubman Boulevard. We will have bypassed Diana Restaurant on Broad Street, and later, Rooster and Relda Cinema on Tubman Boulevard in Sinkor. By the time we make the final left turn on to Sinkor Old Road, I will prepare to get off the bus. Just as we pass the 'transformer', I will holler, "Bus stop!" When the bus stop, I will get off and pay my fifteen cents to the carboy. I will watch him toss my fare into the pile of coins in his *magic* washcloth, bang on the side of the bus and then skillfully hop on as the bus takes off.

"A hungry man eats with a hefty appetite"

African parable

Palm-Butter Rice, So Sweet!

When shall I see my home?
When shall I see my native land?
I will never forget my home!
Palm-butter rice, so sweet! Oh yes!
Palm-butter rice, so sweet! Oh yes!

They say that the way to a man's heart is through his stomach. Some men, I believe, would prefer cash; it would even travel faster. Palm-butter Rice? That's another story. First of all, for a highly anticipated dish of palm-butter rice, you refrain from using the word 'cook'. You must say, 'steam'. One would tell you that a steamed dish of palm-butter rice would travel to your heart faster than lightning would. Liberians cook Palm-butter like they invented it. We even sing a song about the dish. That's how powerful it is. Here's to the heart of the matter.

It begins with a trip to the market. Your list takes account of numerous precious ingredients: bonnie, dried fish, fresh fish (barracuda is a definite winner), meat of any kind (dried deer meat would kick it up a notch), palm nuts, kiss-me (*these are small clams that are shaped somewhat like Hershey's Kisses; only slightly longer. Liberians refer to it as kiss-me*), crab, pig's feet, crawfish, cow's feet (*perhaps the best set of feet that has ever carried a cow*), pepper (hot billy-goat pepper), onion, chicken soup (maggi cubes), salt, palm-butter leaf – not the leaves from the palm tree, and poo-si-wa (*parboil*) rice or country rice. Quite frankly, you may add or take away ingredients to your liking. If you are fortunate to acquire "paddy rice" from the farm, it will elevate the value of this dish to a level beyond any man's dream.

You get to the market by taxi, bus or 'mandigo car' (*you walk*). Remarkably, people walk about the busy market without bumping into each other. It does not take a special skill to work your way between those tightly placed tables. One acquires this skill from the many trips made to the market during one's lifetime. Some people even balance their basket or pan on top of their heads while walking. This is not to show-off. It is to free their hands. To foreigners, this skill gives the impression of coolness; especially westerners.

The boisterous market place is indeed enticing. Persuasive market women (*merchants*) would lure you to their wares for what they claim to be the best goods available there. "Good friend, come buy my bonnie," they will call. Or, holler "Fine bonnie, here! Fine, fine, bonnie here!" You finally choose the merchant that is most convincing or loudest and ask, "How much?" Of course, she will tell you a price a little higher than the actual cost. Why? It is because everyone bargains at the market. No one pays the first price that is told to them – *Beat the price down.*

Buying from one market woman after another, you carefully select your ingredients as you go down the list. Pinch the palm nut with your fingernail. If it bleeds red oil, its pulps are juicy. Pay for the number of piles (*neatly separated portions of about 40 to 50 palm nuts*) that you want. She will funnel an old newspaper to put your palm nuts in. These market women are generous. She may even dash (*tip or add*) you extra kernels.

When its time to buy your rice, should you need some, in your mind, you inspect the measuring rice cup. You know that besides beating the bottom inward she may have also waxed the inside. These generous market women are also polished dealers. You will not get an accurate measurement of the visibly large Mackerel can she is using. You do not complaint; you are used to it. You buy two extra cups to make sure that you have enough rice. She too may dash you. Collect all of your ingredients and place them in your basket or pan. Balance it on your head or not and head on home.

Preparation is demanding - simply put. You commence with heat, using a coal pot or an electric range or a gas range or the ever-present three-stone fireplace. All of your ingredients are washed – nothing is sealed at an 'open' marketplace, remember? The palm nuts are washed and put in a separate pot for boiling. Fresh fish carries the burden of scrapping the scales off the body, splitting the belly to remove the guts and gills and cutting it into large chunks. Besides the minor pricks from the fins, it's not so bad. These enter the pot last; you don't want them to break up. The tail of the *kiss-me* is chopped off with the use of a cutlass or a rock. Use the dull side of your cutlass; otherwise, you could break the blade. Crabs and crawfish are cleaned, and later ripped into smaller pieces. To keep the smoked flavor of the dried bonnie, wash and boil it with the skin attached. It will be detached before being added to the rest of the ingredients. Did you know that the broth from this could be use as a seasoning? Sure you did. The single pot holding the meat, dried fish, bonnie, crab, kiss-me, etc, is the start of something 'superior'. When salt, billy-goat pepper, maggi cubes and onions are added to season the pot to taste, the aroma is breathtaking.

It is now time to steam your rice. Bring your rice water to a boil. Wash the rice, twice or three times and drain the water. Hand feed your boiling pot with the wet rice grains. Cover your pot to cook. Give it enough time to steep. The rice crust has its devotee. If it's "new rice", I'll take it. Dogs love it! There are no finicky pets in Africa. Trust me.

By the way, did you also believed that if you had rice grains in your bed, when you went to sleep, it ran after you in your dream? Possibly that tale was told by a clever parent who did not want the kids to eat in the bedroom. It later spread to every kid I knew.

The time finally arrives to add your most important ingredient - the sauce from the palm nuts! Drain the water and empty the cooked palm nuts into your mortar. Get your pestle and briskly pound the pulp off the kernels. This causes you to sweat. On the brink of completion some dramatic sweat beads will gradually come into view on your forehead. When you are finished, be careful when empting your mortar. NEVER, I insist, use your hand to empty your mortar; especially with your fingers pointing upward and rubbing against the walls of the mortar. SPLINTERS! Use your cook spoon (*serving spoon*) to remove the battered palm nuts, put it in your pan and add some water. Water added to the battered palm nuts will develop into a partially-thick sauce. You may want to put the chaffs through several wash. Get the entire pulp! With the use of a sifter, pour out this wonderful sauce into the 'superior' pot. Don't forget your palm-butter leaf, it embellishes this dish's distinct aroma. Cover your pot only to a bare opening and let it simmer to the moment of great delight. The bubbling of the boiling sauce momentarily jolts your curiosity. Remember what they say about a 'watched pot'? It never boil.

Prepare for your grand presentation. On a tray or dinning table, you will neatly place your steaming rice. It appears so inviting, it sits like a queen next to her king. Then, close to the brim of your soup bowl, this lusciously thick reddish sauce practically covers every piece of mouth-watering ingredient used to create this wonderful flavor of a king. Compliment this dish with an icy cold bottle of Club Beer or Coca-Cola. Voila! Your dish is ready to be consumed.

The ingredients will not guarantee you the result. I couldn't tell you the secret to 'tasty' steamed palm-butter rice. It is in the hands of the one who prepares it. However, I can assure you that your anxious tasting buds will appreciate the eloquent taste of this dish, so skillfully prepared, you will forget the grueling hard work put into its preparation. Palm-butter rice, so sweet! Oh yes!

"Pestle can never hurt dumboy's back"

Liberian parable

Tough Love

The *rattan* is a flexible bamboo about the size of an adult's pinky finger. It is the ever so unpleasant guest in most Liberian homes. Every time your parents brought one home, it would mysteriously disappear. The thing about it is, it also mysteriously resurfaces when its need arrives. Would you believe people made a living selling those things at the market? Who were these people? Chastise advocates? Oh well, I get the feeling there were well-behaved children in those homes. Then again, who knows, aren't kids defying?

When your parent asked, "Where is my rattan?" and if you were the central character in that drama about to unfold, it's like this: for some strange reason, should the ground was to open and swallow you up, it would seem your lucky day. Every child foreseeing a justifiable punishment would agree. We did not particularly care for those moments, yet we did not always obey our parents' rules.

And, what made us believed that if you put a stone (pebble) underneath your tongue your parent would not remember to whip you? My sister, Akitee, tells me that it worked for her two out of five times. What were your odds?

What one parent would consider a reasonable punishment, to another it would not be. The manner in which *some* Liberian parents scold their children may seem a bit harsh, but it was tough love. Some techniques may be questioned. Whether or not you agree, it was because they wanted us to be productive citizens. I believe *that* was their reason. Without a doubt, Liberians love their children.

In our home, the harshest punishment any child received was the switch/whip or the belt – you got a good whipping which, in my opinion, was always justified. We earned every one of them. If I may say so; my parents, to an extent, were lenient. God knows I got away with plenty. Sorry Mom.

29

The kind of discipline used is base on the disobedience or naughtiness. Scolding went from your parents, especially your mother, quarreling to a much painful method. Believe me, sometimes you do prefer the harsh punishment than hearing your mother quarrel for hours. On a serious note, some of these punishments are no laughing matter. As far as I am concern, they were all harsh. Take for instance, *pumping tire*. You place your pointier fingers in both ears and went, rapidly, from a standing position to a squatting position repeatedly. At times, this lasted for about thirty minutes.

Another punishment, to *pick pin*, which in my opinion, was more severe. You stand on one leg and lean forward until you touch the ground with your pointier finger. You remain up side down for the length of time instructed. I guess they did not think about the blood rushing to your head or was *that* the punishment?

Remember '*so ni don*'? The word 'humiliation' comes to mind. This punishment was for a bed wetter. They dress you down in old clothing and take you around the neighborhood while the kids bang empty cans and sing this song:

So ni don
Gbay my donna
So ni don
Gbay my donna

Talk about brutalizing one's self-esteem. The whole thing doesn't make sense to me anyway. I guess folks thought by humiliating you, you would stop wetting the bed. I wonder if that ever work? What if the child had a weak bladder, would humiliation cure it?

The one punishment that I hated the most was *peppering;* the use of hot pepper. Maybe it is because of my intolerance of this spice. Some parents smear hot pepper over the entire body of the child. I do not know how best to express my hatefulness for this punishment. How about - Unthinkable!

The infamous punishment, to *cut jacket,* was not so bad. The playing field is dead even. This is when your parents have become fed up with fights between two siblings and refereeing has gone past annoyance. The two involve will each bring a rattan or a belt to exchange licks. You take turns striking each other with the rattans until you both begin crying. I suppose parents loved this punishment. They saved their energy and siblings gain respect for one another. I am sure that this punishment either prevented future fights or parents never heard about them.

Harsh punishments? Well, they seem so. On the other hand, no one died because of any of those punishments or had a near death experience. We, as children, respected authority; whether you were at home, at school or the neighbor's. We never used the word, 'lie', we said instead, 'you're telling story'. You did not suck your teeth (*to hiss*) at anyone either. Those were considered cussing. Cussing was prohibited in *every* approach. Profanity - out of the question. We did not swear, period. We honored our elders and we knew 'our place'. 'Our place' granted us the luxury of being cared for, being loved and being protected.

For those of us who do remember, one thing is certain; Liberia hardly had juvenile offenders.

*"If rain does not fill the bucket,
can dew fill it? "*

African parable

Games We Played

Mama: Children, children I call ya'll
Children: Mama, Mama we don't care!
Mama: I send my dog behind ya'll
Children: You send him we will kick him!
Mama: I send my switch behind ya'll
Children: You send it we will break it!
Mama: I send myself behind ya'll!

After hearing enough 'back-talk', the child playing the role Mama would then run after the rest of the children until someone is caught. The child that is caught would then play the role of Mama.

The world sat stunned at the athletic abilities of the African teams at the World Cup 2002 games. We Africans weren't. Visit any neighborhood in Africa; you are more than likely to see two young boys play "Butt" – that is when one child head butts the ball thrown at him by another. These are skills that professional footballers acquire to make a name for themselves.

Our early days of the trendy comradeship that we shared came about thinking up ways of creating memorable moments. I do not know the origin of these games. We learned them by watching our older siblings and were later included as we matured. We entered deals with each other (*you both lock your pinky fingers together and one of you karate-chops it loose*) and these deals were governed by strict confidentiality. Never tell your parents should you get hit or are dispossessed of your belongings because you got caught off guard. Here are a few: (1) *free ke ke,* you must remember to keep your rear end covered with a hand otherwise you get kicked. "Free kick". (2) *bufet, ground hold it,* when your belonging is knocked out of your hand and falls to the ground. You lose whatever it is to the other person that knocked it out of your hand and says, "bufet, ground hold it." (3) *fee-on,* you must keep two fingers crossed at all times and show it when the person says to you, "fee-on", and (4) *green leaf,* you must have in possession a green-colored object with you at all times, preferbly, a green leaf.

The main thing is, if you are caught off guard, you will be hit and/or lose your possessions, be it your dinner or a toy or your snack. No matter what the consequence was, you could *never* report it to your parent. We also spoke in code, ***I-pay say-pay that-pay***, to share secrets or gossips with our best friend. Those who did not understand the spoken code had no clue as to what was said. You say "pay" after each word. That wasn't so difficult.

Whether it was Salala, Careysburg, New Georgia, Sanniquelle, Plonkor or New Kru Town, every Liberian child values his or her playtime in its friendly neighborhood. We hopped, jumped, butted, ran, or climbed. One way or another, we had fun. Games we played were life lessons, and we did not even know that. Take for instance, "As I was passing by", it gives an advise that as an adult, I take serious. It went like this.

> *As I was passing by,*
> *My aunty called me in*
> *And she said to me,*
> *O (your name), take time in life,*
> *(Your name),take time in life,*
> *(Your name), take time in life,*
> *(Your name), take time in life,*
> *You've got far way to go.*

And we ended it by swinging our hips and carrying on, *Oh rock it, rock it, shoo, shoo. You rock it, I will shake it, you shake it, I will rock it.* I don't know whether it is because of that game that I take precaution in doing things, but I do.

What about, "Train, train, drop it"? We form a circle holding hands, one person takes a handkerchief and run around the outside of the circle, drops the handkerchief at the foot of someone who is to chase them around the circle until they reach the spot where he or she was standing. If he is not caught, (the one who droped the handkerchief) than the person, at whose foot the handkerchief was dropped, becomes *it*. We sang and clapped our hands.

34

Train, train drop it.
I wrote a letter to my darling,
On the way, he dropped it.
Little boy picked it up
And put it in his pocket.

When I think about that song, I often ask myself, did the boyfriend deliberately dropped that letter? Mmmmm... Something to think about.

The notorious *Na Foe!* - The game of all games. Don't be surprised by anyone's sole desire to get you on his or her side if you are considered a 'master'. Some were even master cheaters. They were good at 'sticking foot'. Children would fight over you to be on their side. Our parents hated *Na Foe*. It was because we beat our feet so often and so hard against the ground, our shoes did not last.

Zeke Salo Ma was not as bad as *Na Foe*. The only problem was our footwear became dusty. To play *Zeke Salo Ma*, we hopped back and forth, clap once and salute with one hand. The other person tries to guess which hand would be used to salute with. If you guess right, you become the lead. You remain in control until someone guesses correctly which hand you use to salute with. For some reason, many children got enjoyment out of this game. I didn't.

I liked the song we sang about the Monrovia boys. Ahhh...those charming Monrovia boys. I guess they were being gentlemanly in helping the young woman reclaim her candy.

I bought my one-cent candy
My one-cent candy fell down
Monrovia boy picked it up
Ah! Ah! Ah! What is this?
Ah! Ah! It's your birthday!

Other games we played were *Bend down to the bush*, *Ya'll leave my pepper bush* and *I declear war*.

Not every home had a television set, but if you had one at home, it was turned on at 6:00 PM and went off at mid-night. There

35

was no 'day-time' television. We preferred playing out doors rather than sitting in front of a TV set anyway. Then again, who had time to watch TV when you had some serious studying to do? Our teachers had their "license" to whip us when we failed a class or did not know our spelling or 'times table'. Play to your heart's content, but when the street lights came on, you had to be home with your books open. God forbid if you had to repeat a class or go to summer school. Your parents would remind you how poorly you did should they even hear you laugh. Tuition, books and uniforms were costly. They did the worrying and we kids had not a care in the world. Kids were compelled to make good grades.

In our neighborhoods, children played with one another and parents watched each other's kids. It did not matter whether your parents were home or not. You always behave as if they were. Whenever an adult neighbor told your parents about something you did, they took their words for it. We had no need for babysitters because parents were instinctively responsible for each other's children. Some even carried out extreme discipline, as in whipping. When that happened, you wouldn't tell your parents either because you might get a second beating for the same thing. In our neighborhoods, we loved each other and life was tolerable!

How I Like My Pawpaw

Tropical fruits are exotic, wouldn't you say? Take for instance the smell of a mango or a pineapple; their fragrance is delightful. I do not believe that Pawpaw, on the other hand, has that trend. Only, its daring breast-like shape can never be mistaken. Either way, pawpaw can rightfully claim its place among those exotic tropical fruits. How do I like my pawpaw? Very ripe.

Other than having the pawpaws to satisfy your own desire, I couldn't tell you any other reason for planting those pawpaw trees I saw around the neighborhoods. There was always a pawpaw tree somewhere in someone's backyard. I do not believe that pawpaw was ever sold at the market. Folks got them for free. I know that I did. All I had to do was ask the neighbor, whose yard the tree was standing, if I could pick one.

Pawpaws hang from the top of the tree's lengthened trunk as they slowly change from green to a golden yellow color, which confirms it is ready to be eaten. Use a long stick to juke (poke at) the bottom of the pawpaw that you want and hurriedly get out of the way while it speedily falls to the ground. Either do that, or ask a pekin (small boy) to climb up the tree and get you one.

Take a knife, split the pawpaw in half and scoop out the millions of tiny black seeds. Actually, they are not that many. Maybe just hundreds. Then again,maybe not 'hundreds' either, but they are many. Peel the skin off the pawpaw, cut the fruit into chunks and put the pieces in a bowl or plate. If the pawpaw is very ripe, you can scoop it right out of its skin and eat it. That's how I like it.

This fruit also makes a good pie-filling. There is nothing better having than a piece of warm pawpaw pie sprinkled with cinnamon or nutmeg. Yummy!

For those of you who have never eaten pawpaw, it bears a close resemblance to a cantaloupe, but only in texture.

Flag Day

How would you feel should someone tell you that your President would be readily available to observe the parade of school children on Flay Day? August 24ᵗʰ is Flay Day; a date all Liberian children look forward to especially if you live in Monrovia. You begin your drilling practices months before, making certain that you will be perfect saluting *him*. The moment is yours; you lead your fellow students, dressed in your school color, and parade proudly through the city streets until you reach the Executive Mansion; residence of the Liberian president.

Tubman High, my *alma mater*, splendor in their maroon and white, always led the procession of schools. This day cabarets B. W. Harris luxury blue and white, Assembly of God's (A.G.M.) brilliant gold and blue, Adventist Junior High's (A.J.H.) dignified pink and black, and Ms. Wilson's well-behaved students dressed in Demonstration's blue and white. Let's not forget St. Patrick's boys in green and white next to their sister-school, St. Teresa's Convent girls. We were captivated with Cathedral's noble khaki and white, College of West Africa's (C.W.A) patronizing blue and white, Monrovia College's (M.C.) illustrious gray and blue, and Well's radiant black and gold.

Sorry guys, I just can't name every school. By the way, for you folks who do not know, C.W.A. and M.C. are not colleges; these are high schools. Most privately owned elementary schools did not participate. My father always accompanied my younger sisters, Joann and Akitee, while they watched the parade from the sidewalks. They did not participate while attending J. J. Roberts United Methodists Elementary School. Their hearts used to 'burn', meaning, they were somewhat envious. Ha! Ha!

Students from all over Monrovia participated. Some schools presented special units of R.O.T.C. students dressed in military uniforms that did tricks with non-functioning M-16's. Majorettes strutted to the band before them. Definitely, the view of those school colors was astonishing!

My favorite time was after the parade, when students from different schools plan their outing together. It was common to see a group of friends dressed in different school colors walking together on the sidewalks of Broad Street. Possibly they had made plans to see a movie at Roxy or Gabriel cinema. Siblings often attended different schools, so on that day it was a good opportunity to meet your sibling's schoolmates or classmate. You know, finally putting a face to the stories your older brother or sister told to impress you of their friends.

There were other scheduled parades that gave us opportunities to meet and hang out with our friends. July 26th, Liberia's independence day and March 8th, Decoration Day. Other occasions, like our school *talent shows,* where students performed on stage at the E. J. Royce's building or City Hall and were backed by a popular local band (Afro Safari or Moga bands). There were also schools' and clubs' basketball or football (*soccer*) tournaments.

On behalf of every Liberian child, I can sincerely say, his/her "school days" are their best!

Judas! Judas!

We celebrated Easter in churches like other Christians throughout the world. However, punishing Judas, as I like to put it, was an added activity. This was something that the children looked forward to. Adults did not participate. Hunting colorful eggs during Easter was hardly an activity. No eggs. No bunnies. No baskets. We sought after Judas. The man destined to be a traitor. Accordingly, someone *had* to have been the one. Judas betrayed Christ and, for that reason, we took it upon ourselves to punish him.

One 'Judas' per neighborhood was sufficient. Every house did not need to have one. Putting Judas together was a joint venture involving all the children from that neighborhood. They collected an old shirt (long-sleeves), a pair of pants, an old hat and a pair of old shoes. With the use of rags or straws, they stuffed and fashioned an image of Judas to appear as a scarecrow. Similar to building a snowman, certain items, like a pipe, a pair of sunglasses or a hat, was added to complete this project. Judas was put in a sitting position in a chair and placed in the front yard. Judas remained untouched throughout the day.

Close to the end of the day, Friday evening, every child in the neighborhood would get a rattan or break a limb off a tree about the size of your finger and head to the house where Judas was kept. Judas was then beaten, until the rags, from which he as built, was totally demolished. What an uproar it was! Fighting your way through the gang of children to take a lick at him.

I wonder about the origins of certain rituals - the tooth fairy, why we 'bless' someone when they sneeze and literally beating the crap out of Judas. I, like most people, participate without giving it any thought. Punishing Judas? Well.

*"When two brothers fight to the death,
strangers reap their harvest"*

African parable

Our People, One People

Unscramble the words to reveal the rich heritage of Liberia.

1. IDANBG   _ _ _ _ _ _

2. RCN-OGIEBLNAOI _ _ _ _ _ _ _ _ _ _ _ _ _

3. OAGL   _ _ _ _

4. ORLAM   _ _ _ _ _

5. ADMNIGON   _ _ _ _ _ _ _ _

6. IEMDN   _ _ _ _ _

7. RUK   _ _ _

8. NOMA   _ _ _ _

9. AVI   _ _ _

10. EOGBR   _ _ _ _ _

11. LBALE   _ _ _ _ _

12. LEPEKL   _ _ _ _ _ _

13. IGO   _ _ _

14. ISISK   _ _ _ _ _

15. ARKHN   _ _ _ _ _

16. ASSAB   _ _ _ _ _

17. ACLEORNAMRBI-IEI _ _ _ _ _ _ _ _ _ _ _ _ _ _ _

18. AND   _ _ _

Across

8. right away
9. listen up
10. fermented cassava
11. to make afraid
13. a major pest in farms
14. frozen Kool-aid
16. expensive
17. really
19. plaything
20. mouth
22. important older person
24. a private talk or meeting
25. a tip
26. street vendor
29. peanuts
32. stubborn or arrogant
34. attractive or excellent
35. peer
36. to fuss
37. another name for a lad
38. term of respect for an older male

Down

1. machete use to clear bush
2. cunning
3. a roadside restaurant
4. to like or admire
5. pal or friend
6. pounded cassava
7. insult or abuse
12. a form of bribe
13. women secret institution
15. always
17. naughty or playful
18. some time ago
21. a popular tuber used to make soup
23. the end
27. to dress up
28. mixed up
29. cowry shells
30. to pass out
31. skinny
33. an indigenous name for Monrovia

44

Liberian Talk

It's time for a moment of *informal* chatter - Liberian style. Can you understand the words that are coming out of my mouth? Use the clues on the opposite page.

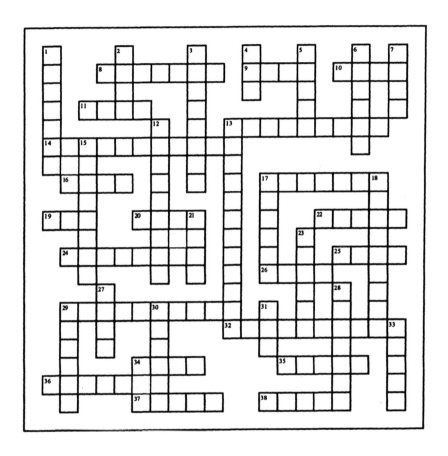

Remember When

Remember when God was head of our homes
And love was the theme we lived
When our hearts were filled with melodies
Of freedom songs and hymns
Kindness kept us going
Neighbors felt belonged
Strangers slept in our beds
And we cradled our children in our arms

Remember at Christmas time
When Sanny Klos entertained us
And Old Man Beggar made us laughed
We drank Club Beer and ate Joll-of-rice
We danced from mid night 'till dawn
We watched the Snake baby dance
And marveled at their acrobatic ballets
We even followed the Gbatu who scared us silly

Remember when school children
Paraded in uniforms to marching bands
Showing school pride in colors and shades
And their ROTC special units did tricks with old guns
We drilled on Flag Day
We celebrated Independence Day

Remember when Liberians were free
Remember when Liberians were kind
Remember when Liberians felt secure
Remember when Liberians were happy
Remember when...

The Mission

Lott Carey, Konola Academy, Ricks Institute, Bromley, Todee, L.T.I. (Luthren Training Institute); to name a few boarding schools where, as a youngster, your independence little by little developed. Some parents sent their children to boarding school at the tender age of eight. Regardless of what age you are, preparation is the same. It begins with your 'list'. Your parents would ask you to make a list of things you will need. The success of this 'list' comes with experience. If you are a 'return student', you will know the essentials. After your books and uniform, your food list quickly follows. Your parents, particularly your mother, will worry about the clothes, blankets and other truly essential items.

Your parents will purchase a trunk or valise, a zinc (aluminum) bucket, a small aluminum tub, an iron, a portable water heater (otherwise you will bath in cold water), and a 'chop box' (a wooden chest). The trunk or valise will be used for your clothes, the bucket, so that you can take your bath, the tub is use to wash your laundry and the chop box keeps your food; mostly dry goods.

Rule number one: He who possesses a chop box also possesses many friends. Rule number two: These friends will last as long as your food last.

Your food list must include gari, sardines, sugar, Nido milk or KLIM, Jacobs cream crackers, Hard Tac biscuits, luncheon meat, corn beef (can), and condense milk. If you have been a mission student for some time now, and you are in grade eight or above, you will sneak a small burner (hot plate) among your things. Of course, this item will be hidden from your parents as well as the dean. Cooking is not allowed in the dorm; but hey, you know the ropes by now. So you will also include rice, Argo oil (cooking oil), chicken soup, salt, a one-quart pot, a plastic plate/bowl and spoons. Your entire shopping for the mission can be done down Waterside.

The dramatic experience of leaving home for the first time is overwhelming. On the way to campus, you sit quietly in the car as your mother gives you her last minute advice. "Study your lesson, don't bring home no failing grades. Take care of your things so that people wouldn't steal them. Stay out of trouble."

"Yes, Mama," you reply, and the entire time your heart is packed with both worry and excitement. You watch your younger siblings unwisely envy you. They don't understand why you could not sleep the night before; but their turn will soon come.

You finally arrive on campus and your parents meet with the dean (overseer for your dorm), who will promise to look after you but never does. Come on, it is impossible to keep such promise; especially when it is made to every parent. They accompany you to your room and at times help pick out your bed. It is your mother who will tend to stay close to you. It is because mothers are sensitive to the fact that you will be homesick. "Make sure you write to us often," she says with a smile. You hold back your tears because there are other students with their parents in the room. You don't want them to see you cry. When your family boards the car to return home without you, you will, more than likely, feel your heart sink down to the bottom of your stomach. If you are very young, what the heck, you go ahead and cry anyway.

First time around for me, I chased the rear of my parents' car for at lest one half mile. I was in the third grade. It seems foolish today, but I was set on catching up with that car and hope my parents would change their minds and take me home with them. Needless to say, that never happened. The best thing about that situation is, I did not go back for the second semester.

Mission life consists of jam-packed responsibilities. That means you use your soap, toothpaste, deodorant and other toiletries sparingly. These items had to last until you went home for a weekend which might be once every two months. You do your laundry by hand, including your beddings, and hang them outside to dry. If you forget to get your clothes off the clotheslines, someone would steal them.

The first year my brother, Aaron, attended school on the mission, he was in the second grade. When school closed, he returned home with an emptied trunk and one pillow. Wow! Can you imagine how my parents felt? I had to mention that.

You attend study hall, a set time used for studying and doing homework either in your dorm or the school cafeteria. If you disrupt the other students during this time, your name is added to a list for punishment. One's name is added to a list for different rules broken. There were boundaries where students were not allowed. If you go beyond a certain boundary, your name is added to a list. If you talk after the lights go out (at bed time), your name is added to a list. If you do not do a chore assigned to you by your *Prefect* (a junior or senior student whose in charge), your name is added to a list. Get the picture? They made all sort of rules that you had to obey or get punished.

Punishment would include cleaning the bathroom, sweeping the yard or cutting the grass with the use of a hoe or a choppier (a machete with a craved blade). These chastisements interfered with your social time. You were not permitted to take part in certain student activities. While the students were social gathering, you were doing your punishment. Would you believe that some students' name would be on more than one list?

I would like to go out on a limp here - Not to mention any names. My cousin, Tannah and my sister, Joann; their names were always on more than one list. Oops, I said their names, didn't I?

Attending boarding school is a life experience you appreciate when you become an adult. The period of separation from your family is awful. You are given rules and punishments, and you go through homesickness and all, but the reward outweighs the, every now and then, moments of unhappiness. You make friends that last a lifetime. You experience your first kiss; perhaps meet your future spouse. You encounter strangers who become family. Best of all, you learn to shoulder responsibilities.

To us those 'mission rules' seemed pointless. We did not understand that our teachers, deans and principals were not just

49

instructors, but *acting* parents as well. They were there to mend a teen's troubled heart, or give prep-talk to a young girl getting her period for the first time, or a young man's inability to cope with peer pressures. The fact is, those rules prepared us for the future when we became adults.

Our growing pains were not so bad. We had schoolmates who helped us along the way. Upper classmates took full responsibility of our needs and guarded us to do the right thing. They were our *play-Ma, play-Pa, play-brother* or *play-sister.* You were always a part of a mission family. Your play-Ma encouraged you to study, cared for your things and taught you how not to be wasteful. I will forever be grateful to my play-Ma Cynthia, who was the 'wind beneath my wings'. I appreciate my mission Ma and sisters; Cynthia, Dell, and Theo.

Boarding schools are expensive. A good reason, I believe, that our parents sent us to boarding school was to teach us independence. They wanted the best for us. They should be truly complimented for their immeasurable love and sacrifices. How would you explain the sacrifices made by these people? On a monthly income of less than two hundred dollars, they bought us books, uniforms, food, clothes and shoes. They paid our tuition (school fees) and provided us our every need. Some parents accumulated far less than two hundred dollars a month; yet, they provided all those things for their children. Would you believe that some family's income was only fifty dollars the entire month? How about that? We owe our parents more than gratitude. We owe our parents our lives – simple as that.

Christmas Season

Children in Liberia know that it is their parents who give them Christmas presents, not Santa Clause. It does not snow in Liberia, so there is no need for a sledge. Our homes have no fireplace, except for the three-stone hearth that is used for cooking in some kitchens, so Santa will never come down a chimney. In my opinion, Christmas is *the* most celebrated holiday in Liberia. Everyone, no matter what your family's financial circumstances are, gets something new. Everyone.

I do not know whether there is a set date, but everyone knows that Christmas season has began with the appearance of the first *Sanny Klos* (Santa Clause). It might be a cool evening, early in December perharps, when at first you barely hear the throbbing drums at a distance. Then, before long, to your delight, the small gathering of strangers eventually reaches your neighborhood; Sanny Klos appears. He is skinny, custom-dressed with sequence trimmings down the side of his pants as well as his long-sleeved shirt, gloves to cover his hands and a pleasant-to-look-at 'false face' *(face mask)*. He is accompanied in the midst of musicians geared with drums, a carpenter's saw, a few empty Club Beer bottles and an old wooden washboard. These musicians pound the drums, strike the saw with the use of a knife and repeatedly run the spoon up and down the washboard to make authentic music. Sanny Klos dances to the rhythm of their beat and performs all sorts of acrobatic turns. He position his body close to the ground, as if he is about to do push-ups, then trembles so we be in awe of the dynamic actions of the trimmings on the side of his pants and shirtsleeves. Spectators pay them nickels, dimes, quarters, and at times a dollar, for their magnificent performances.

I can assure you that this entertainment gets addicting. Absentmindedly, you tend to follow the group as they leave your neighborhood. The show is so incredible that you are not aware of the distance that you have traveled as they go from one neighborhood to another. Before you know it, you have gone several miles from home without your parents' permission.

51

Many children got into trouble because of this. I always got into trouble following Sanny Klos beyond places my parents did not allow me to go. But my parents did not always go 'tough love' on my little behind. They know how it is. They were kids at one time.

Beside Sanny Klos, Old Man Beggar also comes along. We loved Old Man Beggar as much as we loved Sanny Klos. Old Man Beggar has a potbelly, dresses in rags and wears a comical 'false face' (face mask). Old Man Beggar did not give you the great performances like Sanny Klos, he or she does as the name pertains. He begs. This is also a much smaller group, perhaps two to three persons, including Old Man Beggar himself. The drummer, who might also be the spokesperson, tells a tale of Old Man Beggar's misfortune trip. "While carrying a canoe full of toys", he tells the audience, "it capsized and Old Man Beggar lost the children's Christmas gifts along with his personal belongings. Distressed over this, Old Man Beggar has to beg for money to replace the things lost" Spectators knew that *that* story was told every year, however they would respond to it as if it was being told for the first time. Everyone even knew the only song Old Man Beggar sang and would always join the musician.

Old Man Beggar! John the Beggar!
Beg for Money! John the Beggar!
Beg for five cents! John the Beggar!
Beg for ten cents! John the Beggar!

Old Man Beggar playfully wobbled his potbelly which made everyone laugh. Spectators offer him nickels, dimes, and quarters as they did Sanny Klos.

There were other groups that toured the neighborhoods to perform. Besides, these are seasonal employment opportunities for some folks. We watched in wonderment at the acrobatic dances of the *snake babies* (young girls between the ages of 5 and 15). Their bodies were attractively painted with white chalk and they wore grass skirts. Flexible and energetic, they amazingly tumbled and jumped flawlessly landing on one leg on the arm or shoulder of their master. At times they balanced their mid-section on a pointed knife that he held. Miraculously there was no sight of blood. They too got paid for their acts as Sanny Klos and Old Man Beggar were. Watching these performances was like being entertained at a Broadway theater, only it all happened in our very own back yard.

Another group of entertainers were the *Devils*. These are African masked dancers, whether for entertainment or ritual. In this case, these Devils are not to be confused with the western concept of the 'devil'. There were different kinds and each had its own characteristics. The *tall devil* is about 16 feet tall. He walks on stilts completely covered with a raffia-made costume. He is enormously agile, effortlessly going low to the ground then rising to rooftop level with equal ease. The *short devil* (the Gbatu), incredibly, changes his height from a three-foot individual to an eight-footer. The *Vai devil* is dressed with tiny mirrors over his entire body. We were frightened by these different characters, but at the same time entertained.

With all these distractions during the Christmas season, thank God school was closed. We would have followed these performers rather than study. If you were promoted to the next grade with good marks, you were guaranteed a wonderful vacation. On the other hand, if you had to repeat a class or attend summer school, it would be a miserable one. Your parents' friends who visited your home would always hand over a five-dollar bill for making good grades. That would be your 'Christmas'. That was a lot of money for a kid. You could take the bus to Broad Street for fifteen cents and see two movies for a dollar and fifty cents. Perhaps buy some peppermint candies or popcorn and a cold bottle of orange Fanta. You would also easily make friends.

On December 25th, Christmas day, everybody would be dressed in a new outfit and, by all means, eat a hefty meal. That was how we celebrated Christmas!

"No matter how the night,
the day is sure to come"

African parable

Liberia, A Cry For Peace

Our freedom-wings fly heavy among common thieves;
They become our leaders
And their greed holds us captive.
In death our voices were silenced
And poverty among us
Stinks like the bones of a corpse.
Now we must live with our children among strangers;
This is the harsh reality of our lives

But I have a burning fire inside of me,
So rebellious and so intense;
If they are caught off guard
By my profound desire for peace,
It is with my pride that I must gamble my life.

Stand by me, beloved Sisters!
My dear Brothers, embrace these complexities!
We must define for us a new path
And must exit every corrupted social institution;
Greed should no longer hold us captives
Because I have a burning fire inside of me.
Let it be contagious!
Let it burn in all of us!

This, I Remember

Just for fun, how many words can you fine? Search for the words horizontally, vertically, diagonally and backwards; then circle them.

Bomi Hills	Jina	Pepper soup
Cassava	Joll-of-rice	Rubber farm
Chop box	Juke	Saniquellie
Corn row	Kitale	Sassa
Cutlass	Kola	Suehn
Dumboy	Lappa	Sweet mother
Eddo	LEC	Tapeta
Eh so	Mamba Point	Tourgborgee
ELWA	Milk candy	Vai
Farina	Monrovia	V-ring
Geigba	Okra sauce	
Head tie	Palm butter	
Humbug	Paramount Chief	

```
K U D B B T C P U E E L K O E Y N T N B
T V A I O B W J Z A L U C I B H A P O F
V R P A M O A A J L O W X T T P S L Q E
X U V W I E S V N O B M A H E A V O T I
O B E A H D S A A K A L E T K C L J O H
B B R Q I R A S U M G T A X U N B E U C
P E M K L I S S B N L M P T E H T R R T
O R M I L K C A N D Y A L T D E E E G N
H F T H S U P C U N L A M H J U C H B U
C A K I A O Z G I M S A E E O S U T O O
R R Z Z I B G J B S M I P A L Z A O R M
T M T N R I G U I O L H E D L C S M G A
A C T P S Y T I N L F U P T O O A T E R
G O E M V T D R E H D M P I F R R E E A
N V E L E H O U U G U B E E R N K E H P
I D D R M V Q X P A M U R C I R O W T N
R C D K I I C G X N B G S I C O A S I K
- N O A N I V Q X I O E O E E W J U K E
V E H A U C P G U J Y V U L L A P P A X
E S S Q K I F A R I N A P F X C K O Y W
```

The Lone Star Forever

Edwin James Barclay

When freedom raised her glowing form
On Montserrado's verdant height,
She set within the doom of night,
'Mist low ring skies and thunderstorm
The star of liberty
And seizing from the waking morn,
Its burnished shield of golden flame
She lifted in her proud name
And roused a people long forlorn
To noble destiny

Then speeding in her course
Along the broad Atlantic's golden strand
She woke reverberant thro' the land
A nation loud triumphant song
The song of liberty
And o'er Liberia's altar fires
She wide the Lone Star flag unfurled
Proclaimed to an expectant world
The birth for Africa sons and sires
The birth of liberty!

Then forward! Sons of freedom march!
Defend the sacred heritage!
The nations call from age to age
Wherever it sounds 'neath heavens arch
Wherever foes assail
Be ever ready to obey
'Gainst treads on and rebellions front
'Gainst foul aggression in the brunt
Of battle lay the hero's way
All hail! Lone Star, all hail!

The Lone Star forever!
The Lone Star forever!
O long may it float over land and over sea
Desert it, no never!
Uphold it, forever!
O shout for the Lone Star banner,
All hail!

"If a man is given thanks for what he has done,
he will have the strength to do more"

African parable

Ma Hawa's Cookshop
Serving Boiled Cassava with Fish Gravy

Food preparation in Liberia is like lovemaking. I will leave that to your imagination. Needless to say, the exquisite taste of a well-prepared dish is indescribable. You must taste it yourself before you dare rebuttal. Uncover a delightful dish of perfectly fried fish smothered in tomato-paste gravy and tell me that your mouth wouldn't water. Or, the aroma will certainly take your breath away. But before your tasting buds begin watering, let me whisk you back to the humble beginning.

More than likely, all of your ingredients will be bought at the market. Except for those who have a cassava garden at the back of their house and do a little fishing from time to time. I think that it is easier to go to the market.

You would think that cassava fish would go nicely with this dish, for the obvious reason, but red snapper is best. First, prepare your fish for frying. Remove the scales, gills and guts, and then cut your fish into med size pieces, about half the size of your palm. Some people slice an x on both sides – reason is, to have the season penetrate or simply to dress it. Do as you wish. Wash the pieces and drain all the water out of the pan. At this time, use your secret ingredients – salt, pepper, and season salt – whatever you need to make this dish tasty. Let the process begin! Cover the pan and set it to the side. Marinate. Marinate. Marinate.

Get your cassava and remove the outer peel – some people refer to it as the skin. Chop it into chunks and wash it clean. The cassava is part of the root of the plant, therefore it will have residue of soil particles. Add just enough water to cook your cassava. Too much water will make your cassava mushy. No one appreciate a soggy cassava. You don't want that! Cook your cassava just right. Add a dash of salt. While your cassava is cooking, prepare your gravy.

By now, your fish should be ready. Add vegetable oil to your pan and heat. Deep-fry your fish, turning over frequently, to an even brown-fried. In the mean time, get some pepper and onion

– of course, slice your onion- and pound them together in your mortar. *Warning* - don't stir down while pounding your ingredients. A little splash of this in your eyes and you will be crying like a baby. The result of this is a rich colorful salsa-like mix.

Brown a reasonable amount of all-purpose flour in some hot oil, saute your salsa mix, add some tomato paste along with your personal secret ingredients and a little water. Simmer over low heat. The end result should not only smell good, but look good. The thick tasty gravy should sit lazily at the bottom of the oil. Your cassava is cooked, drain all remaining water.

One may serve it as one dish or seperate your cassava and fish gravy before serving your guest. This dish is eaten with the use of a fork. Either a hot or cold drink can compliment your spread.

Palm-Wine in My Belly

Forty years before the Civil War would end slavery in the United States, on February 6, 1820, a 300-ton brig, the Elizabeth, sailed out of New York harbor bound for West Africa. On July 26, 1847, Liberia, Africa's first republic, was declared an independent state. An astonishing phenomenon when the incompatibility of the races made African slaves. You see, there is a certain pride that comes with every citizen about his or her country. This, my friend, is the pride that I treasure. Equally so, because of the tremendous suffering that our society has gone under due to the civil war, that pride sits like palm wine in my belly—sweet yet sour. It is as if we have lost hope and totally forgotten about prosperity. Nevertheless, I remain profoundly proud.

I am proud of our age-old custom of storytelling. It was fashionable. The storyteller would holler, "Once upon a time!" and her listeners would respond, "Time!" Yes, we sat attentively and listened to the voices in African folk tales that entertained as well as enlightened us. We celebrated the voices of romance, the ordinary, the extraordinary, the hero, and at times, the fool. There was always a lesson to be learned. While animals often portrayed the characters in those folk tales, Spider was the most popular character in Liberian folk tales and, at one time or another, has been portrayed with the mannerism of all the above personalities. My favorite tale of Spider is the reason for his tiny waist—greed.

I am proud of Liberia's Angie Brooks, the second woman from any nation, to be president of the United Nations General Assembly. I am proud of Liberia's Edward B. Blyden, one of the first African nationalists whose writings before the turn of the century expressed his belief that Africans should cultivate their own distinctive identity and values. I am proud of Liberia's George Weah, the only player in history to be named European, African and FIFA Player of the year in the same year, 1995 - The world's best soccer player. I am proud of Liberia's Momolu Dualo Bukere, whose authorship in 1814 is attributed to the invention of a syllabic script of 160 symbols, one of only four indigenous African scripts in existence. Mr. Bukere was from the Vai tribe.

In the complex world of our civil war, I still find inspirations in our national seal; an ocean with a ship under sail, to remind us of the long odyssey of our ancestors as well as our accessibility to the rest of the world; a rising sun above the horizon, which symbolizes the birth of a nation and pride in our African heritage; a plow and a shovel in the foreground on the shore, to remind us that Liberians' labor can turn our land's bounty to our sustenance; the palm tree, the source from which the palm oil has enriched us through trades; the white dove, flying with an open scroll in its beak, indicating that knowledge can be spread with peace; and most importantly, our motto: "The love of liberty brought us here."

I am proud that Liberians have lived in a nation which has been independent and self-governed from the get go. I hope that in time to come, every Liberian will be able to improve in every way made possible by God. I believe that pride is there to be claimed by each of our children and us. The Republic of Liberia was founded by Blacks and governed by Blacks for the well being of Blacks. There is no other country in the world quite like Liberia.

*"Advise and counsel him,
if he does not listen
let adversity teach him"*

African parable

I Thank All Of You

God have sent individuals in and out of my life for different reasons, at different times and for different purposes. I thank each of you, from the bottom of my heart, for helping me to grow.

My parents, Jeanette and J. Nostelda Lewis Sr., thanks for your immeasurable love. I could never repay you for your sacrifices. My brothers, Aaron and Jenkins, thanks for your overly protective love. My sisters, Marie, Veronica, Joann and Akitee, thanks for your shoulders to lean on. Pinkie D. Thomas, my 'big sister', thanks for helping me pursue my dreams. M. I. Harding, your support has been a blessing. Audrey and (uncle Joe) Jonathan Sims, since I was a little girl you have always put joy in my heart. Aunty Beck, thanks for the laughs. Pat Molloy, my dearest friend, thanks for your undivided attention to my cries. Cynthia Greene, Theo Daniels and Dell Logan, thanks for taking care of me. Anna S. Wleh, I am glad for your friendship. (Aunt Val) Valerie Morris and (Cousin Almira) Almira Freeman, thanks for the encouragement. My best friend, (Treese) Theresa I. Fletcher, many thanks for the memories we created together. Angela and Robert Taylor, thank you so much for caring, one of these days I will make it to Canada. Augustine Sherman, thanks for introducing poetry in my life. It was you who ignited the spark for my writing. Richard and Samilla Thorpe, thanks for always supporting me in my writing. (Cuz) Paulette Finley, I appreciate your help. (T-Heck) Thomas and Helen Holman, thanks for the support. My godmothers Arimetta "Minty" Holman, I certainly miss you and Beatrice Allen, thanks for your love. Frank F. Holbert thanks for sharing your life with me.

Thanks for your support and cheers: Irene Andrews, Myrtle Bernard, Doughba Caranda, Ms. Thelma Cato, Randy and Versia Davis, Julian Dennis, Nehemiah Dixon, John T. Greaves III, Kemberly Harris, the Holman families, Judith Moss, Will and Mary Oliver, Florence Page, the Ricks families, Mariah Ross, Linda Rush, Joyce Santos, Muniru Sanusi, Shallon *Honey-ice-tea* Smith, Mickey Spencer, Mike Spotts, Tannah J. Swen, the Thorpe families, the Vinton family, and (Uncle D) Derick White.

My *earth angels*: Farrah, Duke, Lemriel, Kia, Benealda, Manseen, Alfreda, Syndi, Malik, Razaq, Kaela and Mylakea, thanks for lighting up my life. Many days your little bear hugs made a big difference.

To all my friends, relatives and fellow Liberians: many thanks for your affection.

Obikai's Heart

Fifteen years ago, Obikai's heart had driven Kpoto to choose love over family loyalty. Now he must find a way to make amends between him and his father before it is too late.

What The Moon Leaves Behind
An African "Cinderella" story

Since Lekani's death during childbirth, her daughter, Seyni, whom she left behind crippled, has found comfort in the arms of Shimita, her grandmother. However, is Shimita's love sufficient for Seyni now that she has grown into a woman in a society that shuns the poor and cripple?

Songs of the Pepper Bird

Can an old man's life experience help save Kamu's troubled heart? Kamu must choose to confess his affair with Baki to her family or risk loosing her forever.

Common Thread

Without her consent, Aku's parents, Aissatou and Nwapa, has found the perfect husband and accepted the dowry. However, on the day of her wedding, 16 year-old Aku must choose between following her heart or following her tradition.

Gowai's New Chief

Chief Kojalu had built Gowai into Africa's most powerful village, now he must choose his predecessor among three men - a wrestling champion, a venturous hunter, and a popular entertainer. But first, each man has to prove his courage. Chief Kojalu challenged the men to travel three hundred miles into the mysterious African jungle and return with a gift impressive to prove worthy of his throne.

Order these titles on line
www.villagetales.com
or
call: (404) 508-0519

The Answers

1. IDANBG	Gbandi
2. RCN-OGIEBLNAOI	Congo-Liberian
3. OAGL	Gola
4. ORLAM	Lorma
5. ADMNIGON	Mandingo
6. IEMDN	Mendi
7. RUK	Kru
8. NOMA	Mano
9. AVI	Vai
10. EOGBR	Grebo
11. LBALE	Bella
12. LEPEKL	Kpelle
13. IGO	Gio
14. ISISK	Kissi
15. ARKHN	Krahn
16. ASSAB	Bassa
17. ACLEORNAMRBI-IEI	Americo-Liberian
18. AND	Dan

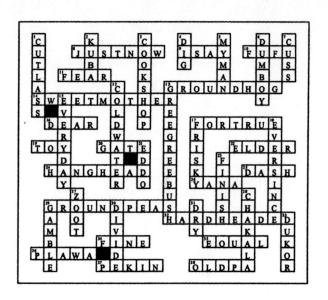

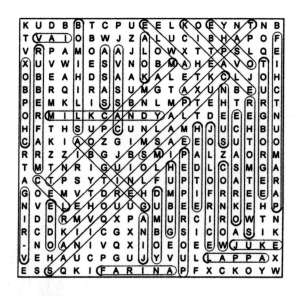